For absolutely nobody.

I WROTE THIS IN EIGHTEEN HOURS, TWENTY-TWO MINUTES AND THIRTY-FOUR SECONDS.

CURTIS WINKELMANN

WITH HELP FROM SUNDAY NEUROSIS

THE FIRST POEM

I

Misery can tell when you're lying. The stern

Truth is an open casket, curtains drawn shut,

— The laughing miserable— all too real,

Those falling eyes as holy water stings the fresh cut.

False, flesh, flung upon Fortuna's wheel,

Whatever lives, already set to die.

The stranded; awaiting time's assault

Running full tilt into a brick wall.

II

A conscious soul is worth a thousand words.

A bitter mirror 's pale reflection, seeking

Everything in absence; a complete null.

For every crack which lines the gold enamel,

Breathes out the width of a true song.

To lie is to love and to live is a lie

The dead no longer suffer, the charade;

A dance performed towards a lighter grave.

III

Ode to the living, who assume they have won,

As one would laugh at his own soul, floating above

The swirling gyres which fuse the moon and sun,

Demolishing all reason in that bare stand-off

Between animal, man and the rational.

The ridiculous rule all, for life is absurd

And death is the only honest event to ever exist.

Not a lonely mode but a hilarious artifice.

IV

Final stanzas like the last breath of life,

So sink deep and think on your memories

Before leaving them behind in something

Flesh filled and cold, and begin to ease

Into the wonders of life, love, death, poetry,

And hope there is more on the next page — or

Close the book and completely regret payment,

The blank white pages of words that never were.

SOMETHING CALLED AN 'INTRODUCTION'

This is a poetry book but I am <u>not</u> a poet. To be brutally honest, I don't believe any self-respecting person should label themselves as one prior to their own demise. In fact, if you are unironically calling yourself a poet in front of your friends and they haven't made fun of you yet I would suggest that you get new ones. They don't truly care about you. So, with that in mind, let's briefly leave the poets in the 20th century and have some stupid, contemporary fun.

Before we begin, I would like to preface this all with an admission: I am a true lover of poetry. I know the more you will read into this book the more it may seem as though I am trying to attack the art but I can assure you that this is not my intention. I am simply just a really bored guy seeking to understand why we resonate so much with the fleeting thoughts of strangers when they are presented in the form of stanzas. And I figured the best way to explore this was through the only way I know how: a really drawn-out, highly ridiculous, pathetic joke.

Within this book I try my best to replicate the depth of serious poetry with no real sentiment behind any of the words. One may use the term 'utter gibberish' to define these subsequent scribbles and I would have to agree. I wanted these poems to exit my mind as quickly as they entered. No internal critic or middleman involved.

In order to complete this self-imposed mission I devised a regimented method of writing. When it came to the semi-serious poems of this book, I restricted myself to a ten-minute writing period in which I could complete the first draft. This left me with no time to plan ahead and thus forced me to write them down with no deeper or profound intent at all. I wanted to see if the stuff that numbly poured out looked in any way like poetry. And if it did, what would that mean? How would I approach my subsequent reading of other people's work? Did I care? Should I be focusing on getting better grades in college? etc.

In regards to the short, comedic poems of this book however, I allowed myself a lengthy thirty-minute time slot in which to tackle them. I wanted them to be funny — at least to me anyway — to make the reading a little less dull and boring. And I have always found that it takes a little more time to come up with something which will make someone laugh instead of cry.

So, what is this book's origin story? Why have I taken up this project? Were my parents killed by a poem when I was young? Is this my revenge? No. But this idea has been growing in my head since I was a child. I have always had this intense anger when engaging with poetry. I'm not sure why but it has always been there. The first time I encountered poetry was back in primary school when our teacher instructed us to read some poems for homework before trying to write one of our own in class. I never understood what was so special about the words on the page. To me, it felt as though we were praising a stranger's lazy thoughts and nothing more. I used to joke around and say that I could write this stuff in a few seconds — not to boast or claim that I was as skilled as these writers but to argue the idea that no matter what I wrote the teacher wouldn't be able to dismiss it as not good enough. You see, up until this point in my academic career there had always been a right and wrong answer to the questions put to us. So, when this assignment came around I was baffled at the fact that our spoofy opinions on nature and our feelings were actually accepted as work.

Even when I entered secondary school and began to seriously analyse poetry in class I couldn't break away from the idea that it was all just shallow words placed into a neat rhyming scheme...or sometimes not — as we were swiftly taught of modernism and the idea that when the poems didn't rhyme and had no structure whatsoever they were actually considered even more impressive. This didn't help with my scepticism. We would be forced to look at Irish poems which found beauty in the mundane — in the housing estates and fields and bins. This infuriated me even more because now I felt as though they were really taking the piss. It seemed to me that these poets weren't even bothered to leave the comfort of their own sofas to come up with their themes and ideas. And I respect the laziness, don't get me wrong, but I own a bin Mrs. Ray — so I really don't need to read about someone else's and why its surrounding flies remind them of the night sky.

Skip forward to college, where I am now greeted with the minds of Yeats, Bukowski, Hemingway and Pound. And suddenly the idea that poetry can be anything becomes a little more profound. But I still naively ask myself, how hard could it be? I mean, obviously these men had great causes to respond to...but could you fake it? Could you just lie about your life and achieve the same effect? I needed to know.

In regards to how I feel presently about the whole situation, I think my focus has shifted from the construction of the writing to its reception. I have found that poetry seems to reach the modern individual's early morning instagram story before their heart. Poetry seems to have become a bit of a meme in these recent times. And I know everyone is an artist these days. And that's great. But I also know that everyone is definitely not an artist. I need rules. I like rules. And when there is none there is no standard. How do we know who to mock and who to praise? It drives me insane. But I also don't think about it all that much...

Finally, I think it's important to note that I am a hypocrite, loser and a grumpy young man. There is no doubt about that. But despite all of the cynicism and ridiculousness which lies at the heart of this book I hope you're still able to find something in here which will make you smile. But not laugh. Because as we all know, those who laugh out loud at books are a bit fucking odd.

— Love, Curtis.

THE BOWMAN'S PEAK

why should i walk to her with heavy eyes

and misery, or allow myself to

be lead to the place where at the real men rise?

i do not recognise this fine, dark part of you,

which blames Troy for Helena's mistake?

what heart becomes my own, or which soul lays

separate, wired and alone and permanently awake?

when Gods are angry it is clear they create.

like feet buried in the sand, they watch the waves

take over a solid root, with the ways of past and gone

she still watches Byzantium fall and burn before her eyes,

our home and place now rubble and dust,

the Gods have us punished,

and we have learnt nothing.

WAKING UP, REALISING IT'S SUNDAY AND THAT I ACTUALLY DON'T HAVE SCHOOL

these faceless apparitions of posterity and doubt:

a murdered lie uncovered by a

wandering

truth.

THE SORROW OF MY NIPPLES

the doomed, holy fire in the resting swell,

the lone, tortured Grecian in a dying heat,

with all generations awaiting hell,

there is no promise of any defeat.

a mournful, white flag raised up into the skies,

which seemed the cruelty of the world in its truth,

neglected melody of painful disguise

and honest monuments of tattered youth;

become, and then immediately swell,

an unaging lover upon a paling heat,

with all the marriages coming from hell

there is never victory in accepting defeat.

PEEL HERE

those *'peel here'*

stickers on food packaging

are designed to drive

the good men mad.

they want us to kill our neighbour

with the unopened

package of grapes

in our hand.

the plastic

wet

from the sweat

of our fingertips.

.   .   .

it's been slightly torn

but in the worst way.

it has been *'peeled here'*

but nothing has opened.

let me get the blade.

the blade solves everything

except pain...

ON BEING ASKED TO WRITE
SERIOUS POETRY

one must admit that pure depth is simple

and therefore, shouldn't really be taken as truth.

but instead, a hint into a stranger's mind;

all are sprawling opinions formed freely

in the moment, with no real care for the time.

adults, once again, talking down to our kind.

PROFESSIONAL ROMANCE

in love

as i lie

stupid flat

on my back

in her chair.

the bright light

casting an angel

in silhouette

while she roots

through my mouth

looking for three

more ways

to make me gag.

. . .

steel instruments

and unloved children,

useful in the dull

damp basements of

the white house.

i cough a little

to breathe,

spraying my saliva

heavenwards.

her glasses covered

in my Sunday mist.

she smiles

a perfect grin

before tilting my head

to the left

and allowing

the pools of blood

and spit

to drain

to the edges

of my jaw.

her plastic hand

resting against my cheek,

softly.

this is the first time

a woman has touched me

in this way

in a long time.

she holds a mirror up

over my head

and i stare at the reflection

placed next to her.

we make a cute couple;

my mouth gaping

and her fist

shoved to the back of my throat.

i hope

she thinks

i'm beautiful

or this will all have been for nothing.

when it's over

she forces me to

make promises

i can't keep while

she bills me for her time

and asks me to leave.

my bite marks

and blood juice

still fresh on her fingers.

evidence

of the complicated affair

which exists

between me and my dentist.

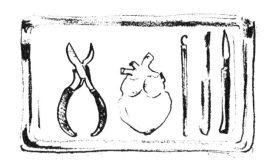

ON THE INSIDE

a pretty woman with a broken bone,

a mother, a liar, a token friend;

bleeding through their teeth.

lies which crack and reshape

your skull like pieces in a jigsaw.

a caring judge, a nurse, a cheater

who stole your lover's heart

and replaced it with something weaker.

you've got your;

wife beaters, smart deceivers,

your lover leavers and child conceivers.

your fifth class teacher and her

husband's bald head.

the bored priest and the sick old man.

your favourite junkie, celebrity and singer

on every street corner, the artist with no talent

and the handsome thug

holding up the charity shop worker

just for fun.

a corrupt official, a normal bloke and

a silent model who does what their told.

the only boy, the every boy, the chameleon

and the class clown; born to be a star and dying slowly.

your old boss and his fat son;

a bully to a classmate who cries with his mum;

a divorced woman left to rot like her pet,

put down then revived and

going on fifty-six in dog time.

the second, third and fourth coming of Christ,

a murderer proved innocent

for the eighth consecutive time.

the person she killed; the brother, the bass player,

a romantic who loves breaking hearts.

millionaires, messiahs and murderous spies,

a war veteran trying his best to survive

while his alcoholic friend fucks his wife

and raises their child.

a harsh comedian falling for

someone who can't take a joke.

a writer, a fraud, and an artist in an empty shell.

men without,

soulless boyfriends, happy husbands

women who love men

they've never touched.

the writer, the fraud, the loser on show.

everyone is beautiful,

or so I'm told...

FOOD ECONOMICS

you know what i hate;

when you're minding your own business

and someone says they made you food.

and you think:

'well, that's kind of you.'

but then

when you're finished eating

they turn to you and say:

> *'would you mind doing the clean up and put away —*
> *in fairness, i was the one who made the food.'*

but you see,

i never asked you to.

in fact,

had i known that was the deal

i would have just starved myself

rather than eat your — let's be honest —

pretty fucking average meal.

DUMP BUCKET

i'm a dump bucket.

open me up

and dump in all the shit

you produce;

the ideas,

the art,

the worries,

the opinions,

the jokes,

the turn-ons,

the turn-offs,

your favourite brand of cigarette

or sex position,

your filthiest story,

your biggest regret,

the way you felt,

the way you should have felt,

the reason you didn't.

dump them all in

till i'm full

and overflowing and choking

and spilling.

till i'm pushing it all back up

and out

and into your face.

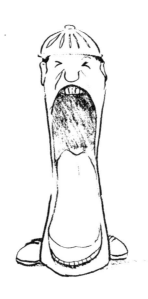

THE 12-HOUR CLOCK

the nerve of you to assume that

i know whether it's six in the morning

or in the afternoon,

because i wish i instantly knew

whether i've slept out the entire day

or if i am about to…

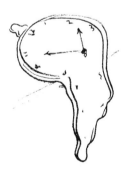

LOVE AND DEATH

if you love something

set it free

and if it comes back to you

it's meant to be.

BUT

if you hate something

kill it with an axe

and if it comes back to you

it's a 100% a zombie apocalypse.

BESTIE

this is my best friend.

i love my best friend.

i only have one and this is it.

the one and only.

everyone else I know

is not my best friend

and if I called you so

it wasn't true.

i was lying

because this is my best friend,

right here.

look at them.

all the rest of you

are frauds.

i said look at them you fools!

this is my best friend.

i'd fucking take a bullet for this person

whose name I believe is…Stephen?

'soy Ricardo'

my god damn fucking best friend, Ricardo.

till death do us part

or, you know —

till tomorrow.

FASHION

monday afternoon hungover

and i'm just glad i have friends

who will buy me a pint without

a knife in the back.

all of the pennies which lined

the pockets of my chinos

sink down into my

brown suede shoes.

i am weighted.

i am wearing jack & jones.

i am the system. i am conformity.

fear me.

yesterday i decided to burn all of my clothes
and start over.
this will be my fifth attempt.
i worry about my own style from the closet
to the dart to the bar we stumble into
after hours.

why did i choose this combination of garments?
because i think i'm someone i'm not.
i saw Brad Pitt wear this in British vogue
so it should look great.
only problem is
i shop at H&M not Tom Ford
and i still have my own face.

however, while i wade deep in the worries
of my own style
i look across the bar and
notice a man in cow print trousers
and a black tactical vest.
maybe there is hope for me yet.

leave me here and in my worries

forever and ever,

amen.

LIFE IN BLACK AND WHITE

life in black and white

because

where is the colour in all this?

through the looking glass she dove

and emerged in a wonderland of allusion.

the desert of the real has you now

wrapped up in a neat little package awaiting

to be delivered on to the next place.

the meeting point of heaven and hell

has always been earth;

the bridge between two sides

of one divine relationship.

visions of cobblestone pavements

and stained glass window fronts

through which you glimpse your being

as it steam rolls past,

leaving your senses behind.

drink this, sit here, feel that

and then

don't.

then lie dead still for eternity and

let the ground reclaim

whatever it was you were.

let the colour drain from you

in a black and white way

and hope you are happy when it does.

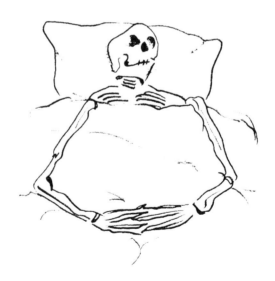

MODERN INSULTS

i've noticed

that these days

insults have become

questions;

> *'DO YOU THINK YOU'RE HARD?'*
> *'WHAT ARE YOU AT PRICK?'*
> *'THINK YOU'RE FUNNY, YEAH?'*

always leaves

this awkward silence

which requires me

to think of an answer.

JUST INSULT.

and stop trying to start a conversation.

THE TRUTH

the truth is sweat and guilt

and laughing with a person

you don't find funny.

the truth is you never grew up.

grown ups don't hang up.

true men don't give up.

GUESSWORK

a lot of people

think that i am fine

when the reality is

i am actually blind.

if i look at you

and i say *'hi'*

that's just me

trying being kind

because the truth is

i can't see you at all.

.   .   .

just guessing and hoping

that the blurry figure

whomst i am waving at

knows me well enough

to say 'hi' back.

THE FASTEST MAN IN THE WORLD

i must be the fastest man in the world

because when i walk on sidewalk pavements

there is always someone in front of me.

i catch up to those who are ahead

which forces me to take a risk in

the abstract art of death.

stepping out onto the main road

instead of waiting,

and overtaking these strangers

in a place they would never think to go.

some crown it impatience,

some crown it intelligence;

but you need to be quick to live life.

there is a slowness in this world so great
i can sometimes taste it in my morning
spit.

it wont kill you
but dying would rip its power
right out from under it.

ignore it and it will leave
a shiny anger in your bones.
i'm bound to attack a pedestrian
or shoot a messenger any day now
and no one will know why.

i must be the fastest man in the world,
that's the only explanation
for this choreographed ballet
of treading heels and bubbling infuriation.

send me away to the olympics,
so i can bring home the gold

and finally make my brother proud.

i must be the fastest man in the world.
i must.

and as time grows old
i heard it spins faster,
leaving the sane people to wonder
where the last twenty years of their life went.

well, i can tell you where at least eight of mine
slipped astray;
stuck behind the slow strangers of this world
who are always in the fucking way.

MIDNIGHT AIR CONDITIONER

i sat with a tired drunk

in a bar

at 12:00 in the night

across from Merrion Square park —

we were trying to flirt.

the drooling hum

of the overhead

air conditioner

was holding my attention better

than her words.

i still can't believe i've been married

to this woman for five olympics now.

i miss my wife.

i try to say a joke but

she takes it as a serious comment.

i don't correct her.

i'm now trapped in a conversation

which is based off a lie.

i have to smile or i'll look dead inside.

she turns and calls the stranger

next to her 'bestie' because she

can't remember her name.

the universe cracks in half.

she reaches out for her glass

with a colourful set of claws

twirls it. doesn't drink.

i know i'm supposed to ask her a question

but all i can think is:

'i guess they really do have air conditioning in hell.'

A FIERCE SMACK ON THE BACK

well,

i guess you win some

and you lose some.

and he lost this time — <u>big.</u>

and will never ever win again.

ever…

i am sorry for your loss.

I AM NOT A LEADER

i am not a leader.

i'm the guy in the back

making fun of the leader's accent.

CURRENT SPIRITUALITY

i believe that everything happens for a reason.

i believe that there is always hope.

i believe that nothing matters.

i believe that everything matters

and I like hanging out with my friends.

i believe that charity is good.

I believe that the world is selfish.

i believe that love is dangerous.

i believe that death is the end

and I like vinegar on my chips.

i believe that nothing makes sense.

i believe that God exists.

i believe that I am God.

i believe that I am insane.

and I like to believe.

JUST FRIENDS

if I get you

and you get me

why don't you get me

and I get you?

why does he get you

and she get me?

why don't we all just agree

to get one another

and then you and me can slip off

and go get each other.

THE LOSER'S FIRST SONG

i start life

crying instead of laughing,

chasing the joke, mouth open

drooling, scared, half-assing.

my language changes

to desperate;

i am loved.

and that is cruel.

what laughs with me

my laugh will devastate.

anything for the joke

and nothing for the weight.

THE INVENTOR OF THE 69

EUREKA!

invert your body

and open up wide

because

we're about to pleasure each other

Orally

at the exact same time.

THE DARK

we're all afraid of the dark

when we're young.

but the harder life gets

the less afraid

we become.

take me and kill me

monster under my bed

i have grown up and found

i have nothing to lose

except the pain and the stress

of exam season blues.

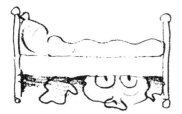 

RELAX, IT'S ART

relax cowboy, it's art.

you can't get offended.

i meant it as a critique

on the idea of the thing

and not the thing itself.

it's both right and wrong

all at the same time.

so you can't bloody touch me

because it's art baby

and no one knows what the fuck is going on.

SGT. PEPPER'S FUCKING MISERABLE

never

take advice

from men

with whole

hearts.

unbroken

and unsure.

seek to

hear about

death

from a

ghost

not a

priest.

A HAPPY POEM

…i got nothin'.

THE SMALL DECISIONS

forever is for all time; for always.

but for me, forever is for as long as i am

and for every day that is,

ever and ever till never comes near.

so, fuck it —

Lisa, i'm havin' another beer!

WRITER'S FUEL

writer's fuel.

a lit cigarette

and a sharp glass of whiskey.

writer's fuel.

i dump the whiskey into my mouth

and light the tip of the cigarette.

writer's fue —

ouchy!

the cigarette has just burned my finger.

ok…

the smoke is now stinging

my eye.

watery — can't

                          see.

fuck,

i'm crying.

oh Jesus,

the taste of the bad whiskey hits.

it's oaky afterbirth

making me gag.

i feel sick.

i'm no writer.

HOMEWORK FOR THE SOUL

i hold my breath

when i walk past strangers

in the street.

always have, always will.

not sure why.

it's hard when

you run into a group of nine

all in single file.

those are the real tests.

purple in the face

just waiting to feel

the delayed gust of wind

which always follows

in the wake of a person

when they walk past you.

count to

three and feel the space

they left behind

begin to fill

back in again.

would you consider thinking

this much

about the moments when a

person will pass you on the street?

i hope you would.

but you probably won't.

you'll probably focus on

subjects like

politics and religion instead.

.   .   .

but i'm telling you,

this is where you will feel

closest with a God.

i find i question existence more

when i'm on the luas

than when i'm staring

up at a clear night sky.

humans in a metal box

moving from one place

to another

for reasons which don't matter

and at the cost of a currency

which we have created

to mean something

extraordinary.

no —

this is definitely where my spirit

does its homework.

in fact,

all that really comes to my mind

when i try and look up

at a clear night sky

is my rapidly deteriorating

eye-sight.

DWAYNE 'THE ROCK' JOHNSON

massive, rich man named:

Dwayne 'The Rock' Johnson,

what does it sound like when you cry?

is it high pitched or is it low —

or is there no sound at all?

does the tear just roll down your massive, rich cheek

and land on your massive, rich chest

quietly?

has anyone ever uttered the words:

'don't cry Dwayne 'The Rock' Johnson,

it will all be alright.'

or do they never ask how you are?

because you're a rock, Johnson

and rocks don't cry,

especially when they're massive and rich —

or maybe they do a rocky cry,

soft and breathless filled with quiet pain.

c'mon, tell us what it sounds like

when you weep Dwayne.

GOOD MORNING!

morning.

for Isherwood, it began with two thoughts:

'am' and *'now.'*

agreed.

sometimes regrettable.

sometimes relieving.

wonder what it will be like

to one day wake-up

and think:

'not' and *'nowhere.'*

SO LONG

so long, farewell, adiós —

i've stopped saying goodbye

and now simply say:

'just don't die.'

because it's true, I don't want that person to die

before the next time I see them.

i could care less about how their bye is

— good, bad or indifferent.

has anyone ever had a truly bad bye?

i'm fairly sure they're fairly good,

or at least fare and well.

and if they are ever indeed bad,

it's rarely classed as a bye at all.

instead, it's just a rudimentary

'fuck off.'

SOMETIMES

sometimes

you just have to take a deep breath

and ask yourself:

'how did I get here?

no wait — seriously,

how did I get here?

who are you people?

and what have you done with my son?!'

y'know?

GROWTH

i'm a 21-year-old man

who still shops for clothes with his mother.

she ends up paying for most of the stuff

and afterwards, we go get ice cream.

i'm an adult

not an idiot.

GUYS WHO DRIVE

guys who drive

get all the girls.

it's a fact.

so hey —

date your taxi driver if you want,

but know that when he parks up

he's just another cant

—ankerous little boy.

(smooth?)

MATURE

don't call me a man

i'm a mature boy.

men take care of the people that they love

but boys love the people that take care of their stuff.

MODERN PHILOSOPHY

if a tree falls in the forest

and no one is around to hear it

does it still post an instagram story

to let everyone know?

GLASS HOUSES AND PAPER STRAWS

it melts away into your mouth

like last night's memories as

you wonder if you're a true hero

because you can't sip your

iced latte without a side mouthful of

soggy, papery pulp.

modern sacrifices for the cross.

are we one hundred percent

sure that this is saving the world,

because i don't feel very super

in my twenty-one year old beer belly

and bleached blond hair.

it's all relative i suppose —

like chewing gum in a cold shower

and hoping it will all work out.

U P

sometimes at night,

i'll look up

and realise it's up forever;

an endless void.

yet,

we'll still give each other birthday cards.

we'll fake laugh at someone's joke.

we'll even throw a smile

to an elderly person

as we pass them on the street —

just so they think that we won't hurt them.

but we will.

THE PLAN

it's easy to be funny

when you train your mind

to go there first.

once, when i was eleven,

i had a girl in my class

come up to me and ask

if i sat down at night

and wrote out

everything

i was going to say

the next day.

an insult in the moment.

'<u>this</u> is the best she thinks i can do?'

but as i've gotten older,

i've learned

to appreciate that comment.

because now,

most times,

i do.

THE BEARDED MAN

it must not be nice

to kiss a guy with a beard.

uncomfortable and yuck.

but i suppose,

guys with proper beards

don't really kiss

they just fuck.

AN IRISH BANK ADVERTISEMENT

we are hope!

we are young!

we are just livin'!

we are Ireland.

it's the cup of tea in the mornings!

it's the up at dawns — no questions asked!

it's the little ones before school!

it's the just about making it throughs!

it's the how do yah do's!

it's a community.

it's the bullshit!

it's the depression!

it's the two public bathrooms!

it's the passive-aggression.

it's the scared politicians!

it's the overloaded bins!

it's the lack of decisions!

it's the new-founded sins.

it's the let's stick together!

it's all the same team!

it's the fucked up weather!

it's the new vaccine.

it's Ireland!

it's the world!

it's human nature to want to survive

by any necessary means.

BREAK IT

i hate to break it to you sir, but you are the joke;

not the words coming out of your mouth

— you.

COMMON GROUND

hospice nurses profit off death.

if death didn't exist then they would be broke.

so, hospice nurses and war lords have something in common?

that's wild…

i'm drunk.

IF

if i told you to you to run,

would you?

if i said i was dangerous,

would you stay?

if i admitted that every word i speak is from a film,

would you care? would you even notice?

i died around the age of eleven.

ever since then this character of me has taken over;

an amalgamation of cliches, scenes, jokes, art

music and opinions.

. . .

if i told you i knew all of this

and still decided to go on living,

would you agree?

i love films

but they definitely fucked me up

to a certain degree.

CARD GAMES WHILE WE DRINK
ALCOHOL

oh, sweet Christ

do I have to play?

or can I just sit here,

sip my drink

and slowly fade away?

I RUSH

at all times

i run to closure

rushing past the moment

to the memories

to relive what I am

and feel secure in

immutable realisms.

evolution has left us with

a distaste for ambiguity.

so even if I do love you,

tell me it won't happen

so it can end and

i can reflect

on why it was

the right move

to move on

from then to now.

MUSIC TIME

keeper of the speaker

may i seek solace in your queue?

armed with the music of my parents

and the hope that you'll lift my mood.

CANON BALL!

blackness and silence.

the sound

of my own breath

forcing itself to exist,

fighting

its way to the surface

in a bubble

and

my thoughts

screaming out

my ears.

. . .

pain

as i lose

the last breadth

and know that

i'll have to return

to the surface

soon.

i don't want to.

i have to

but i do not want t-

A KISS

i'll look deep into your eyes,

shift my body towards yours,

caress your face with my hand

and press my lips to your snout

because you're an aardvark.

PET

there you sit

curled up in my legs,

beautiful and whole.

you're a dog

and i'm just a guy.

i'm a dog person.

are you a human person?

or are you just doing all of this

so that i won't legally kill

and replace you...?

POETRY

yeeeeaaaaaah poetry!

me — writin' the poetry.

you — readin' the poetry.

somebody out there — whackin' one off.

I FUCKING HATE NERDS

i fucking hate nerds

with their nerdy way

and nerdy voice.

why are they like that?

those fucking nerds.

no one else is nerdy like nerds

with their nerdy hearts and nerdy eyes

that'll probably one day

attract some nerdy wives.

they'll move into a nerdy house

and live a nerdy life,

have three nerdy kids

and become a nerdy five.

and their nerdy incomes
from their nerdy jobs
will support their nerdy souls
till they pass on.

to nerd heaven they go
with all the rest
and live happily ever after
doing what nerds do best.

BEING FUCKING NERDS!

NOTHING EVER MATTERS, EVER

nothing ever matters, ever.

that's the matter.

if it mattered sometimes,

then i'd want it forever.

but it can't be always.

so therefore,

ever becomes never

when nothing ever matters, ever.

THE STUBBING; OR ACCIDENTALLY DRIVING MY SMALL TOE INTO THE LEG OF THE TABLE

FUCK! FUCK! FUUUUCK!

FUCK YOU!

FUCK MY WIFE!

AND END MY FUCKING LIFE!

THAT HURT LIKE A BITCH IN HEAT!

YOU INANIMATE FUCKING OBJECT!

YOU LIKE HAVING NO ANIMATE?

HUH?!

...

ANSWER ME!

TWO MAGNETS

two magnets,

the same pole of both

being forced together,

getting close but then

slightly bouncing away

from one another.

we are close too

but we'll never click.

which is fine.

a science necessary

for the world to literally

keep on spinning.

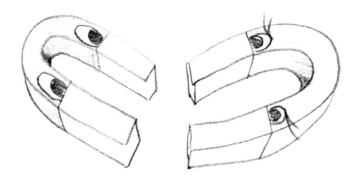

GARY

this moment, only.

THAT'S JUST YOUR OPINION

all life is opinion;

you shouldn't kill people

and we should use money

to buy things.

all i am are opinions.

LOSING LARRY

are there any more Larry's

left out there?

where did they all go?

little Larry's loving life;

laughing at the fact they are all called

Larry.

did all the Larry's leave

to look for love?

or is no one called Larry anymore

because of that child molester?

I AM COOL

i don't talk too much

and i don't know your name.

i'll give you a fist-bump bro

instead of a handshake.

things work out for me

even when i don't try.

so suck it world

i just get by.

THE COLOUR BLIND KILLER

'what's your favourite colour, Chris?'

'what's the colour of blood again?'

'...red.'

'oh, then dead people.'

THE BIG SILLY HYPOCRITE

look kids!

there he goes again,

the big, silly hypocrite

with long arms down by his side

and a big, bushy beard

behind which he hides.

judging the lives of other people

with soft, sour strokes of his pen.

he is no more different or intelligent

than those who he mocks,

he simply feels better

by criticising the flock.

. . .

a flock that he is a part of

in every single way;

a quirky little fact

which haunts his hollow heart

each and every day.

JIM ON BOYFRIENDS

i just don't understand what they're offering.

i mean

what are they offering compared to

someone who — I don't know —

has a soul?

beer, sip, gulp.

the boyfriend, man.

you know what they are, right?

'a Heineken for me AND a gin for her.'

smoke, light, puff.

that's what they're offering —

a body with no soul.

all of the photographs,

look closely,

they're all in pain.

sip, gulp, puff.

stare at the photographs

for long enough

and you'll see it.

the girlfriend forces that photograph, man.

she takes his soul with it.

witchcraft.

soulless.

beer, sip, gulp,

light, smoke, puff.

i needa piss...

WORK

your only friend

bashes away

at the keyboard

while you sit

curled flat

between the

couch pillows

waiting

for that dizzy

feeling to pass.

the taste of smoke

sits on your breath

and you wait.

. . .

he works

while you wait

and think on work;

plan to it

hope for it

fear only it.

each finger

slamming down

on a key

is a reminder

that you wait.

work waiting on you

while you wait.

CLASS PRESENTATION

oh boy,

it's a class presentation!

so let's just pretend

that i know what i'm talking about

and you're here to listen.

i mean,

you know

i don't know.

and i know

you know

i don't know.

. . .

yet we'll act as though

we care about it all,

when the reality is that

none of us could give

two flying monkeys

about the Indo-Nepal treaty

of the 1950's.

but hey, what'd you say

that for the sake of our grade

we just keep pretending

that this whole dumb process

is worth the air we're expending.

YASSS

'oh my god, yasss queen, i'm so bad!'

it's pronounced Y-e-s

and you are Aimee,

you're living a lie.

this person you're projecting is falsified.

stop speaking in inherited phrases

and common cliches

and actually open the fuck up.

please.

DEAR,

I know there's a lot of pressure riding on you. I've heard so much about you for so long — I mean, a lot. Some good and some bad. Not going to lie, I am expecting big things. I know I for one wouldn't be able to handle the pressures of living up to an expectation. But that's just me. I'm sure you'll do fine. Also — handshake, fist bump or covid conscious elbow touch? Let me know ASAP so we don't kick it off to an awkward start. I am a handshake man personally but I can adapt.

And listen, If I don't end up getting into heaven, no hard feelings. Take care of yourself and I hope the universe turns out well.

All the best,

Curtis.

JUST BE

some people just be.

floating through life

just being to be.

the misconception is that

they don't think of others

but that's simply untrue;

they think of others

but still do as they do.

people like old laundry

drying out in the sun.

blind to their peripheries

and always focused on one.

how do you do it?

how do you not care

about the stardust and atoms

which make up your air?

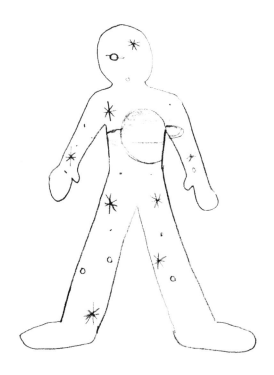

THE AIRPLANE BATHROOM

i wonder who was in here before me?

and why this place is so damn clean,

when i know it's drowned in dried,

misdirected pee?

can everyone out there hear what i'm doing?

will this thing suck me through the piping?

did the doors fold in or out when i entered?

oh look, there's me in the mirror,

in my travelling-clothes and earphones.

> *'i'm really high up right now,'*
> i suddenly remember...

anyway,

time to go back to my seat

and take notice of every single person

who will go to pee after me.

playing their own part in the same

airplane bathroom routine.

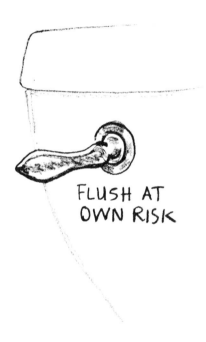

FLUSH AT
OWN RISK

THE SUN

big ball of fire and light

placed right up in the sky.

anyone else seeing this shit?

responsible for all life on earth

but oh yeah — don't look directly at it.

it will burn the eyes right out of your head.

this thing which created us

will eventually leave us dead.

said to blow up in a few billion years or so.

when all i will be is dust and bones.

so good luck with it fellas

let me know how it goes.

LEFTY

i'm always right.

even when i'm wrong i'm right.

even when i'm left i'm right.

even when i'm read i am bloody write.

and don't you forget it, kid.

CURIOSITY

put a gun to my head

and ask me what i think of myself.

i'm genuinely curious.

CAR ALARM

shut the fuck up.

i hear rhythm in your screaming

and now i'm singing along

while my ears are bleeding.

BEEE BOOO BEEE BOOO BEEE BOOO

why do these things do what they do?

why do they even exist?

has anyone ever run to their car alarm and

actually found a thief,

just standing there,

the window smashed and

the wheel in their fist?

.   .   .

"alas, i've caught you red handed sir!"

i would shout.

> *"ok, fair enough"*
> he would then utter.

> *"— but wait, hang on a second, i've a gun*
> *you snot-nosed little fucker."*

he'd shoot me in the chest

and watch me fall,

take my wallet and my phone

and then pull off with a roar.

my neighbour would open up his window

and i'd scream:

"call the police! call the police!"

> *"turn off that fucking car alarm."*
> he'd say.
> *"i can't hear myself think."*

#THEIR INITIALS AND THEIR AGE

stop using this hashtag

when it's somebody's birthday.

no one even knows

who you're talking about anyway.

it's not a national holiday.

it isn't important.

it's just some day

in a month

when someone wasn't aborted.

HERO

this past year

the concept of a hero has been torn apart.

we don't believe anyone can save us anymore

and those who should, are probably evil.

does anybody out there

still believe in heroes?

THE SIZE OF MY PENIS

Large (Women's UK).

?

it wasn't anything, y'know.

but it was something.

to me, it was everything.

to you, it meant nothing.

— dedicated to the guy i went to school with but barely know who got on the dart and saw i had my earphones in and just waved without coming over to strike up a 20-minute conversation about college and the weather.

BEGGARS CAN'T BE CHOOSERS

important to remember that:

beggars can't be choosers.

unless of course

they have a gun…

people tend to get what they want

when they have a gun.

A CONVERSATION

i'll say something

then you'll respond

but with a question at the end.

i'll respond to that question

and end with an exclamative clause.

you'll continue on my point and input your own

experience and opinion.

we'll now have established a report

and can continue on with our lives

never having to feel awkward

around one another when we don't speak,

because we have officially acknowledged

each other's existence

and that seems to be all we seek.

BULLYING INNOCENCE

i saw a kid on the dart

who wore a school bag

as big as him.

one of those red jansport ones

that could solve the housing crisis

if it had working plumbing.

this kid was so innocent.

i remember his type;

nice guy, shy, loves his mum

and most likely bullied.

these kids grow up

but they never learn.

they stroll around college

with the bag so high up on their back

it doubles as a neck brace.

it pulls their whole being

closer to God as

they hang from it

with their canvas shoes

barely grazing the ground.

if you are ever that desperate

to get better posture

just get a girlfriend.

but first you'll need

to lower that bag

about eight pegs, kid.

i wonder how they never notice this.

have they watched any t.v. show ever?

wear your school bag low and

become invisible.

simply aim to survive

and you'll do fine.

EVERYONE IS DOING SOMETHING

look, everyone is doing something!

they're out and about.

they're in and down.

a yellow sun is setting

over a small foreign town.

the is pool blue and their skin is brown.

they're posting videos of themselves drinking

and laughing with no sound —

muted; someone said something risky

in the background, or maybe

they're all just screaming…?

feel jealous

then look at your own life

and feel even worse.

be a part of something

by being apart from it all.

isolated.

live a vicarious life you don't want

with people you don't like

or even know.

then wait till you're invited to do something

yourself

publicise it immediately

and let the others suffer

the same way you once did.

WHAT PAGE IS THIS?

no more wrong answers in a landscape of equality,

but a fresh million of wrong questions.

when you tread, tread carefully

because you tread on my opinions.

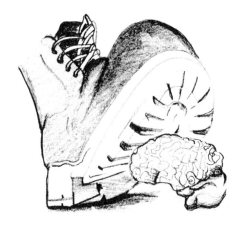

THAT 2AM TAXI HOME

back-seated

in between cheap alcohol

and the passing green, red and

yellow.

ask the cold up front

if there is much business left

for lonely men tonight and

let the darkness talk back,

telling you about his losing

football team, bitch of a wife

and angel of a daughter

who takes after

her mother.

discuss religion and love

and explain why it is

you are not afraid to die

but scared to live.

explain why it is you never

looked her in the eyes

and never said the truth.

why you never told her.

then move on to his brother

who he never sees or hears from.

listen when he tells you he

hopes that he is still alive.

then fall into one another

and begin to cry.

therapy is never easy

especially when it's on the meter.

SHADOW

I WRITE UNDER THE DUBLIN SUN,
THE ARCH ABOVE ME CASTS
A SHADOW DOWN
THE PAGE RIGHT   HERE!
A LINE
OF LIGHT
AND
DARKNESS.

I WRITE ON EITHER
STRADDLING SIDE OF THIS LINE
IT.

AS THE EARTH TURNS,
AND THE SUN MOVES,
So DOES THE SHADOW.
IT BEGINS TO TAKE OVER
THE LIGHT.
NOW THE LINE IS HERE.
SHADOW.
LIGHT.
THE LIGHT OF HUMOUR
AND THE DARK OF POETRY.
I'M CHASING THE LIGHT
BUT THE SHADE IS WINNING.
AND I'M NOT BRAVE
OR CONFIDENT,
So I GIVE IN TO THE DARK.
BECAUSE IF YOU CAN'T BEAT IT
LET IT SWALLOW YOU WHOLE.

PASSING PHANTOM

sometimes i think i see you

galloping past my window

on your noble steed.

i believe in simple selfishness

and this is a glimmer of some.

there must be life after death

because you're living one.

THE POWER OF LOVE

please circle an option:

a) create a living, thinking, feeling person from nothing.

b) reduce a living, thinking, feeling person to nothing.

WE THE PEOPLE

there has not been a better example

of youth activism in this country

since fifteen-year-old boys furiously

and unwaveringly fought

in support of 2014's #freethenipple campaign.

honestly inspiring.

A SITUATIONAL COMEDY OF ERRORS

sitcom me.

sick of the con

of life and

hoping to

see the wrongs

i do

through my own eyes

and not sit on the moon

above it all,

looking down at myself

sin on

making the same

mistakes.

but instead,

make a sitcom

a shit song

of the things which

i think about

because if i can't

exist on

the big screen i'll

live long and pretend

i'm strong,

while i build a bomb

of thought and worry

right here.

THE CHOICE

it's night time.

i lye sideways with my brick

lighting up my face in blue

and my hand shoved —

not just into my underwear —

but all the way through.

once again,

forced to make the impossible choice;

do i choose the back of my eyelids

or everything in the history of the world?

THE MOST MANLY MAN IN THE WORLD

he once shot gunned a beer

and then nursed it back to health.

if he said it was christmas

people would start singing carols.

he's interrogated by the authorities

because they enjoy his stories.

he speaks sign language

in Chinese, Thai and German.

women love him, men envy him

and aliens want to study him.

. . .

he tells women what their star signs mean

and enjoys his caffeine black.

when a tree falls in an empty forest

he can hear it squeal,

and sometimes God is left to wonder

if he's even real.

he parallel parked a shark once

while music listened to him.

lonely feels he and when it rains

it's because he' s crying.

poor life decisions make him

and laughter causes him to joke.

he is the most manly man in the world.

there is no doubt, he is so.

THANK YOU

you know when

you're beating the shit out of an elderly person

and they start to cry...

if yes, then thank you for purchasing this book even though you're mentally unwell.

A TALKING MONKEY IN A SUIT STROLLING DOWN A BUSY STREET TOWARDS CAMERA

'the capital city — a living, breathing being.

full of life, colour and laughter.

a hub for the poor

and a playground for the rich.

this is where it all happens.

hundreds of chimpanzees flock to this location

every year.

and what's bringing them? —

bananas.'

THIS POETRY BOOK

i lean back

into my chair

and put my feet up on the desk,

taking a break from writing

this poetry book —

the one you're reading right now.

i check my phone and a

girl who i used to know pops up.

cool.

she's happy and posing

with a boyfriend.

he's happy.

they went away together.

so,

it's serious

i guess.

i look at them

posing together.

happy and away.

and then i look at me;

my feet up on the desk,

leaning back into my chair,

trying to write this non-sensical

poetry book because

why the fuck not.

i won't tell you who won in the end

but i'm sure you've figured it out by now.

GOD

sometimes i wonder if i am God.

i wonder if God knows what will happen before it does.

i wonder if he slept in a bunk bed till he was 20.

i wonder if he feels alone most of the time.

i wonder if he thinks he is funny;

if he can tell a joke to fill a silence and avoid a feeling.

i wonder if God thinks he is insane

and if he is too old to be where he is.

i wonder if he knows where his father lives.

i wonder if he regrets losing love or

if he is even capable of it at all.

sometimes i wonder if i am God.

DO IT YOURSELF

FLIRTING

why hello there…

tell me,

did it hurt when I fell from my apartment window?

THE END?

life is making you laugh,

everything else is just waiting.

…but as God said, crossing his legs, I see where I have made plenty of poets but not so very much poetry.

— CHARLES BUKOWSKI

ACKNOWLEDGMENTS

Family and Friends, I know you don't want anything to do with this book but this is the section in which I thank you all the same.

— Curtis

ABOUT THE AUTHOR

Curtis Winkelmann is not a writer nor a poet. Yet, he has created this book within a couple of hours in the hope that it will make someone out there a little less bored.

instagram.com/curtiswink

Printed in Great Britain
by Amazon